LEVEL
3
Fact Reader

Ink!

100 FUN Facts About Octopuses, Squid, and More

Stephanie Warren Drimmer

NATIONAL GEOGRAPHIC

Washington, D.C.

For Blake and Molly —S.W.D.

Designed by Yay! Design

Library of Congress Cataloging-in-Publication Data

Names: Drimmer, Stephanie Warren, author. | National Geographic Society (U.S.)
Title: National Geographic readers : ink! / by Stephanie Warren Drimmer.
Other titles: Ink!
Description: Washington, DC : National Geographic Kids, [2019] | Series: National Geographic readers | Audience: Age 6-9. | Audience: K to Grade 3.
Identifiers: LCCN 2018057780 (print) | LCCN 2018058867 (ebook) | ISBN 9781426335037 (e-book) | ISBN 9781426335013 (paperback) | ISBN 9781426335020 (hardcover)
Subjects: LCSH: Cephalopoda--Juvenile literature.
Classification: LCC QL430.2 (ebook) | LCC QL430.2 .D75 2019 (print) | DDC 594/.5--dc23
LC record available at https://lccn.loc.gov/2018057780

The author and publisher gratefully acknowledge the expert content review of this book by Janet Voight, associate curator of invertebrate zoology at the Field Museum in Chicago, Illinois, and the literacy review of this book by Mariam Jean Dreher, professor of reading education, University of Maryland, College Park.

Photo Credits
AL=Alamy Stock Photo; NGIC=National Geographic Image Collection; SS=Shutterstock
Cover, Kondratuk Aleksei/SS; header (throughout), Potapov Alexander/SS; 1, Steve De Neef/NGIC; 3, David Liittschwager/NGIC; 4 (UP LE), Narchuk/SS; 4 (UP RT), David Shale/AL; 4 (CTR), Koji Sasahara/AP Photo/Tsunemi Kubodera of the National Science Museum of Japan, HO/SS; 4 (LO LE), Fisheries And Oceans Canada/SS; 4-5 (LO), David Liittschwager/NGIC; 5 (UP), Paulo Oliveira/AL; 5 (CTR LE), Chris Gug/AL; 5 (CTR RT), David Liittschwager/NGIC; 6, Kondratuk Aleksei/SS; 7 (UP), Kristina Vackova/SS; 7 (LO), Demkat/SS; 8, Bertie Gregory/NGIC; 9, Sergey Popov V/SS; 10 (LE), Ethan Daniels/SS; 10 (RT), Carrie Vonderhaar/Ocean Futures Society/NGIC; 11 (UP), wildestanimal/SS; 11 (LO), Victor R. Boswell, Jr/NGIC; 12, Stocktrek Images/NGIC; 13 (LE), Greg Dale/NGIC; 13 (RT), Millard H. Sharp/Science Source; 14, BrendanHunter/Getty Images; 15 (UP), Fred Bavendam/Minden Pictures; 15 (LO), Jeff Rotman/Nature Picture Library; 16 (LE), Sompraaong0042/SS; 16 (RT), Rich Carey/SS; 17, Roberto Nistri/AL; 18 (UP), Alex Mustard/Nature Picture Library; 18 (LO), William West/AFP/Getty Images; 19 (UP LE), Fred Bavendam/Minden Pictures; 19 (UP RT), Jeff Rotman/AL; 19 (LO), Dante Fenolio/Science Source; 20 (UP), irin-k/SS; 20 (LO), Dorling Kindersley/Getty Images; 21, Conrad Maufe/Nature Picture Library; 22-23, Rich Carey/SS; 23, Michael Greenfelder/AL; 24, Lachina; 25 (UP), J.W.Alker/AL; 25 (LO), Kjell Sandved/AL; 26, Agarianna76/SS; 27, Carlina Teteris/Getty Images; 28-29, Paulphin Photography/SS; 29, bluehand/SS; 30, Vittorio Bruno/SS; 31 (UP), NaniP/SS; 31 (LO), Steve Trewhella/FLPA/SS; 32, Dr. Roger T. Hanlon; 33 (UP), sha/Getty Images; 33 (LO), Borut Furlan/Getty Images; 34-35, Magnus Larsson/Getty Images; 35, Ethan Daniels/Stocktrek Images/Getty Images; 36 (UP), David Fleetham/AL; 36 (LO), abcphotosystem/SS; 37 (UP), Mathieu Meur/Stocktrek Images/Getty Images; 37 (LO), orlandin/SS; 38 (UP), Mike Veitch/AL; 38 (LO), Mario Pesce/AL; 39 (UP), Jak Wonderly; 39 (LO), atese/Getty Images; 40, SEA LIFE Kelly Tarlton's Aquarium; 41, Britta Pedersen/EPA/SS; 42-43, Furzyk73/Dreamstime; 44 (UP LE), Vibrant Image Studio/SS; 44 (UP RT), Brandon Cole Marine Photography/AL; 44 (LO), David Liittschwager/NGIC; 45 (UP LE), Carrie Vonderhaar/Ocean Futures Society/NGIC; 45 (UP RT), Julian Stratenschulte/DPA/AL; 45 (CTR), Robert Sisson/NGIC; 45 (LO), WaterFrame/AL

**National Geographic supports K–12 educators with ELA Common Core Resources.
Visit natgeoed.org/commoncore for more information.**

Printed in the United States of America
19/WOR/1

Table of Contents

25 Cool Facts About Cephalopods   4

Chapter 1: Aliens of the Sea   6

Chapter 2: Odd Bodies   14

Chapter 3: Brainy Behavior   28

25 More Facts About Cephalopods   44

Cephalopod Facts Roundup   46

Index   48

1
Some squid can glow in the dark.

2
Cuttlefish pupils are shaped like a *W*.

3
The piglet squid has a see-through body that makes it nearly invisible to predators.

4
Like sheep, goats, and toads, octopuses have rectangular pupils.

5
A live giant squid was photographed at the ocean's surface for the first time in 2006.

6
At the ends of its tentacles, the colossal squid has hooks that can swivel.

7
Deep-sea squid often eat one another.

8
Pygmy squid are so small that they often cling to blades of seagrass.

9
A deep-sea squid called the octopus squid is known to detach its arms to distract predators. (It later regrows them.)

10
Dumbo octopuses get their name from their large fins, which resemble the ears of the Disney-movie elephant.

11
One type of squid called the odd bobtail squid shoots out glow-in-the-dark mucus instead of ink.

12
Some species of young squid gather in groups of thousands, called schools, to stay safe from predators.

25 COOL FACTS ABOUT CEPHALOPODS

13

Newborn cuttlefish are so small that four of them could fit inside a teaspoon. But they can already hunt and make ink!

14

Striped pajama squid spend most of their day hiding under sand on the seafloor.

15

When threatened, the blanket octopus unfurls long sheets of skin attached to its arms in order to appear bigger.

16

Dumbo octopuses live deeper in the sea than any other octopus—up to 23,000 feet below the surface.

17

After eating, many octopuses pile the empty shells of their prey outside their den.

18

The lyre cranch squid has eyes on long stalks.

19

The deadly blue-ringed octopus is the size of a golf ball, but it packs enough venom to kill 26 humans within minutes.

20

In certain light, a vampire squid's skin and eyes look deep red.

21

One ancient cephalopod had an 18-foot-long shell— that's longer than an SUV!

22

One captive octopus was so fond of a Mr. Potato Head toy that he fought back if anyone tried to take it away.

23

Mother octopuses carefully guard their eggs and gently push water over them to give them oxygen.

24

The deep-sea cockeyed squid has one bulging eye that sees shadows in dim light and one smaller eye that spots animals glowing in the dark.

25

The cockatoo squid holds its arms together, curved over its head, which makes it look a bit like the bird it's named after.

CHAPTER 1

ALIENS OF THE SEA

Octopuses have THREE HEARTS—and blue blood!

Octopuses, squid, and their relatives are so weird, they're almost like aliens! They use their long arms to catch prey and their sharp beaks to gobble them up. Many can shift their shapes and colors, and even squirt clouds of ink.

Cuttlefish sometimes seem to HYPNOTIZE THEIR PREY by flashing colors and patterns.

And they're some of the most intelligent animals in the sea. These creatures are called cephalopods (SEF-uh-luh-pods).

A squid's brain is shaped LIKE A DOUGHNUT.

Cephalopods' arms are ATTACHED TO THEIR HEADS.

In fact, "cephalopod" means "head-footed." Cephalopods are a group of sea animals related to snails and slugs. They're invertebrates (in-VUR-tuh-brits), or animals without bones. But all cephalopods have a hard beak. They live in the ocean all over the world.

Let's meet the cephalopods!

Octopuses have eight grasping arms and soft bodies that can squeeze into tight spaces. They are so smart that they can steal lobsters out of traps and learn to solve puzzles.

Octopuses can usually fit through ANY SPACE LARGER THAN THEIR BEAK.

Squid and cuttlefish have eight arms, plus two longer tentacles (TEN-tuh-kuls). When they're not hunting, they keep their tentacles tucked away.

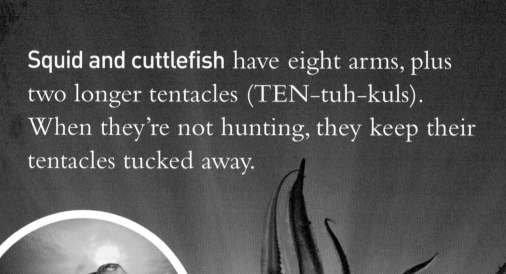

Squid have
TUBE-SHAPED BODIES,
while cuttlefish have
SHORT, BROAD
BODIES.

Nautiluses are the only cephalopods with a shell. The shell is divided into chambers, and the animal lives in the biggest one. When it gets too large for the space, it grows a new, roomier chamber and moves in.

chambers

Cephalopods dominated the seas for 400 MILLION YEARS—more than TWICE AS LONG AS DINOSAURS ROAMED EARTH!

Around 550 million years ago, most ocean creatures could only crawl along the seafloor. Then along came cephalopods, some of Earth's first swimming animals. In time, they took over nearly every corner of the seas and became the ocean's most fearsome predators.

Scientists have discovered the fossils of about 17,000 EXTINCT CEPHALOPOD SPECIES.

There are more than 800 SPECIES OF CEPHALOPODS alive today.

THERE ARE NOT MANY FOSSILS OF OCTOPUSES because their soft bodies don't preserve well.

Then, about 65 million years ago, they were almost wiped out. It was from the same worldwide disaster that killed most of the dinosaurs. But a few species survived. Over time they became the cephalopods that share our seas today.

CHAPTER 2

ODD BODIES

An octopus can TASTE WITH ITS SUCKERS.

Imagine being able to taste and smell with your fingers. An octopus can, by using the hundreds of suckers on each of its eight arms. The suckers are also so strong that they're able to rip apart crabs and clams. But they are incredibly sensitive, too. They can fold in half to delicately pinch small bits of food.

The largest OCTOPUS SUCKERS CAN EACH LIFT UP TO 30 POUNDS—the weight of an average three-year-old!

A giant PACIFIC OCTOPUS has about 2,000 SUCKERS.

The edges of an octopus's suckers have MICROSCOPIC GROOVES that help FORM A TIGHT SEAL.

15

All cephalopods rely on their flexible limbs to explore the world and find food.

Besides their eight arms, squid and cuttlefish also have a pair of long, thin tentacles tipped with suckers or hooks. When they find a tasty fish, they snap out their tentacles, grab it, and yank it into their mouth.

tentacles

Nautiluses have no arms, only tentacles—
more than 90 of them! Their tentacles are
covered with grooves and ridges, instead
of suckers. A sticky glue helps them hold
on to food.

Tiny to Tremendous

← This is a close-up view of a pygmy squid.

← A boy checks out a giant squid on display at the Melbourne Museum in Australia.

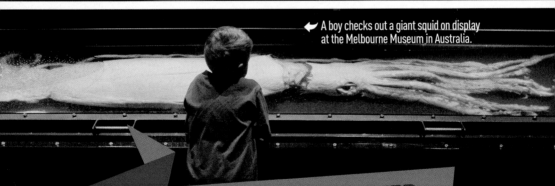

The pygmy squid is so small IT COULD FIT ON YOUR FINGERNAIL—while the giant squid can be LONGER THAN A CITY BUS.

a newborn giant octopus next to eggs

a full-grown giant octopus

Cephalopods come in all sizes. Some even go from itty-bitty to enormous in a single lifetime! The giant Pacific octopus is one of Earth's fastest-growing animals. It hatches from an egg about the size of a grain of rice. But in just three years, it can grow up to 20 feet— the height of a giraffe!

One newly discovered tiny octopus species IS SO ADORABLE that scientists may name it ADORABILIS.

FEMALE ARGONAUTS— a type of octopus— can be 600 TIMES BIGGER THAN MALES.

In the depths of the ocean lurks a creature of truly monstrous size. At nearly 43 feet long, giant squid are the largest invertebrates on Earth. But they live so deep underwater that they are hard for scientists to study.

The giant squid has the WORLD'S BIGGEST EYES—they're BIGGER THAN SOCCER BALLS!

One thing we do know: Giant squid fight whales in epic undersea battles. The whales are often found with circular scars on their skin from squid suckers, and with huge squid beaks inside their stomachs.

The legendary SEA MONSTER CALLED THE KRAKEN may have been based on the giant squid.

This giant squid washed up on a beach in Tasmania, Australia.

Mighty Movers

Cephalopods don't swim the way fish do. Instead, they move by jet propulsion—the same force that powers rockets! They suck water into the muscular sacs that form their bodies. Then they blast it out at high speeds through a narrow tube called a siphon (SYE-fun). By adjusting the position of their siphon, cephalopods can control which direction they go.

In addition to their siphons, some cephalopods have FINS THAT HELP THEM STEER.

siphon

Japanese flying squid can JET RIGHT OUT OF THE WATER.

Nautiluses have a special way of moving. A nautilus shell is made up of many chambers. Each one is sealed and holds gases inside. This allows it to float. To move down, the nautilus can inject fluid into its chambers through special tubes. Or it can suck fluid out to float back up. It's the same way a submarine works.

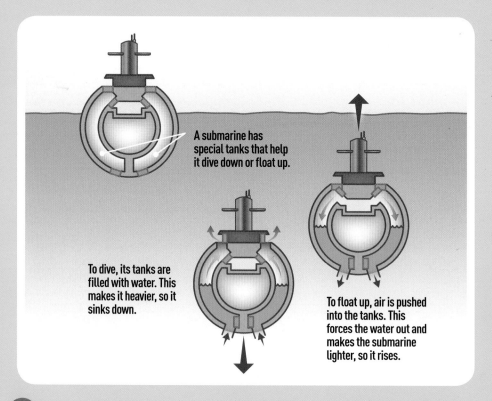

A submarine has special tanks that help it dive down or float up.

To dive, its tanks are filled with water. This makes it heavier, so it sinks down.

To float up, air is pushed into the tanks. This forces the water out and makes the submarine lighter, so it rises.

NAUTILUSES USUALLY SWIM BACKWARD, with their head and tentacles trailing behind them.

Chambered nautiluses have such a strong shell that they can DIVE DEEPER THAN 2,000 FEET WITHOUT BEING CRUSHED by the pressure.

A 600-POUND OCTOPUS can squeeze through a tube THE SIZE OF A QUARTER.

Captive octopuses sometimes CLIMB INTO OTHER TANKS AND EAT THEIR NEIGHBORS.

In the wild, octopuses' ability to fit into small spaces helps them wedge into tight hiding spots. In aquariums, it makes them expert escape artists. Late one night in 2016, an octopus named Inky sneaked out of his tank through a small gap. He plopped to the floor and slithered across the room to a drainpipe. Then he slid down the pipe, which led to the ocean— and freedom!

Octopuses sometimes CRAWL OUT OF THE WATER TO HUNT.

CHAPTER 3

BRAINY BEHAVIOR

Most of an octopus's BRAIN CELLS aren't in its head—they're IN ITS ARMS.

Scientists think octopuses USE LANDMARKS TO FIND THEIR WAY HOME.

Each octopus arm has a mind of its own. In an experiment, scientists cut off an octopus's arm. (Don't worry—octopuses regrow their arms.) The detached arm kept seeking out food. It even tried to put food where the octopus's mouth should have been!

Among invertebrates, CUTTLEFISH HAVE ONE OF THE LARGEST BRAINS for their body size.

Cephalopods' brains are very different from our own. But these animals display many smart behaviors, from fooling one another to playing tricks on their keepers.

Masters of Disguise

Many cephalopods SQUIRT INK to CONFUSE PREDATORS.

Most cephalopods store ink in a sac inside their bodies. When threatened, they release a blob of it, then jet away. Sometimes they create ink clouds that look like their bodies. That can fool a predator into attacking the ink instead of the creature itself. Tricky!

Cephalopod ink contains a chemical that experts think may IRRITATE PREDATORS' EYES AND NUMB THEIR SENSE OF SMELL.

cuttlefish eggs without ink

Some cuttlefish ADD INK TO THEIR EGGS to help hide them.

cuttlefish eggs with ink

In one experiment, cuttlefish MIMICKED A BLACK-AND-WHITE CHECKED PATTERN that scientists put in their tanks.

Cuttlefish, squid, and octopuses can change their colors whenever—and however—they want. These cephalopods have special cells in their skin that contain a colored substance called pigment. When they squeeze or relax muscles around the cells, the cells shrink or expand. This lets them create all kinds of patterns, including spots and stripes.

↑ In this black-and-white photo, a cuttlefish imitates a human-made pattern.

reef squid

Squid can change their colors FOUR TIMES IN A SINGLE SECOND.

A cuttlefish's skin has more than 20 MILLION PIGMENT-FILLED CELLS.

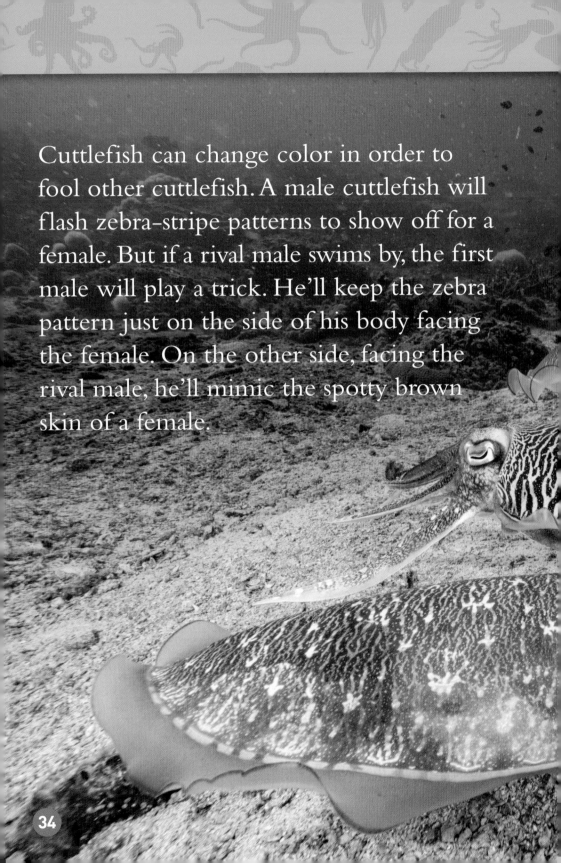

Cuttlefish can change color in order to fool other cuttlefish. A male cuttlefish will flash zebra-stripe patterns to show off for a female. But if a rival male swims by, the first male will play a trick. He'll keep the zebra pattern just on the side of his body facing the female. On the other side, facing the rival male, he'll mimic the spotty brown skin of a female.

To scare away predators, cuttlefish sometimes put A PAIR OF SPOTS on their back THAT LOOK LIKE EYES.

fake eye

mimic octopus

The mimic octopus CAN IMITATE MANY DIFFERENT SEA CREATURES, including stingrays, lionfish, and sea snakes.

sea snake

Some octopuses and cuttlefish can change more than just their color. They are covered with tiny bumps called papillae (pa-PIL-ee). They can use muscles to reshape their papillae to change the texture of their skin.

By holding their arms in just the right way, they can change their body shape, too. One second, they can be round like a rock. The next, they're branching like a coral.

Mimic octopuses protect themselves by POSING AS DANGEROUS ANIMALS, like stinging jellyfish.

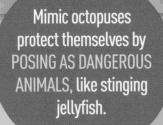

Pharaoh cuttlefish will MAKE THEMSELVES LOOK LIKE HERMIT CRABS to help them sneak up on their prey.

Some octopuses will use six arms to IMITATE A CLUMP OF SEAWEED, while using the other two arms to walk away from danger.

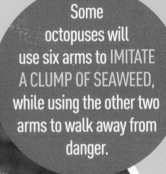

37

Clever Creatures

Veined octopuses sometimes CARRY COCONUT SHELL HALVES TO USE AS A SHELTER when predators come near.

Some scientists believe that CUTTLEFISH CAN COUNT. In a study, cuttlefish chose five shrimp over four, and four shrimp over three.

SOME OCTOPUSES PILE UP ROCKS to block the entrances of their homes.

Veined (VANED) octopuses are the first invertebrates known to use tools. That makes them one of just a few animals on Earth that have this ability, including chimpanzees and dolphins. Many scientists consider tool use a sign of intelligence.

Another sign of intelligence is the ability to learn. Rambo, an octopus at a New Zealand aquarium, learned to snap pictures of visitors with a camera placed in her tank. Octopuses can also learn to find their way through a series of tunnels and unscrew jars to get a treat inside. Octopuses can even recognize individual people. They'll crawl toward keepers they like—and shoot jets of water at those they don't.

Cuttlefish can SOLVE MAZES.

↑ Rambo uses her camera to snap photos.

Octopuses can learn to OPEN CHILDPROOF PILL BOTTLES.

Cephalopods can even outsmart their caretakers. In 2008, Otto the Octopus got annoyed with a bright light shining on his tank. Every night he squirted water at the light, making it go out. His keepers took turns sleeping on the floor to figure out what was causing the blackouts!

One octopus was known to JUGGLE THE HERMIT CRABS in his tank for fun.

Giant cuttlefish are curious and will often COME RIGHT UP TO DIVERS to check them out.

Scientists are diving ever deeper into the world of cephalopods. These creatures are sneaky and smart. They fool each other and know how to have fun. What will we learn next about these shape-shifting tricksters of the sea?

1

Some squid can swim at speeds of up to 25 miles an hour—twice as fast as an Olympic champion!

2

Scientists have created an octopus-inspired material whose shape and texture can be changed on demand.

3

The average giant Pacific octopus can lay 90,000 eggs.

4

Giant squid use their long tentacles to snatch prey up to 33 feet away—that's almost the length of a bus!

5

The blanket octopus sometimes tears a stinging tentacle off a Portuguese man-of-war and uses it as a weapon to fend off predators.

6

Some cephalopods live in the deepest part of the ocean, where there is no sunlight.

7

Every year, millions of firefly squid twinkle with glowing blue light in Japan's Toyama Bay.

8

Though cuttlefish are known for their color-changing abilities, scientists think they're actually color-blind!

9

Scientists believe that all octopuses are venomous. But most aren't dangerous to humans.

25 MORE FACTS ABOUT CEPHALOPODS

10
An octopus's suckers grab by reflex, but a chemical in its skin keeps the suckers from sticking to the octopus by mistake.

11
To keep them free of fungus, Hawaiian bobtail squid coat their eggs in a jelly that contains bacteria.

12

Scientists are developing a robotic arm inspired by an octopus tentacle to help doctors perform surgeries in hard-to-reach areas of the body.

13
A cuttlefish's eyes allow it to see what's in front of it and what's behind it at the same time.

14
Most adult cephalopods are solitary. But bigfin reef squid group together in long lines, possibly to look bigger to predators.

15

Humboldt squid have been spotted attacking sharks.

16
Most cephalopods live for only a year or two.

17
A cephalopod's beak is similar to a parrot's, but upside down.

18
Most octopuses hunt at night. But the day octopus stalks crabs, clams, and fish in the daytime.

19
Some cuttlefish use their arms to walk along the ocean floor.

20
All cephalopods have a rough-textured tongue called a radula (RA-juh-luh).

21
Nautiluses sometimes eat shrimp and lobster shells to get nutrients that help them grow their own shells.

22
The word "octopus" comes from an ancient Greek word meaning "eight foot."

23
Some cuttlefish hide by burying themselves in the sand so that just their eyes poke out.

24
The two-spot octopus has shimmering blue spots near its head that look like an extra set of eyes.

25
Cephalopods have special organs called statocysts (STAT-uh-SISTS) that help them balance underwater.

CEPHALOPOD FACTS ROUNDUP

WHOOSH!
You've jetted through the cephalopod specifics. Did you catch all 100 facts?

1. Some squid can glow in the dark. 2. Cuttlefish pupils are shaped like a *W*. 3. The piglet squid has a see-through body that makes it nearly invisible to predators. 4. Octopuses have rectangular pupils. 5. A live giant squid was photographed at the ocean's surface for the first time in 2006. 6. At the ends of its tentacles, the colossal squid has hooks that can swivel. 7. Deep-sea squid often eat one another. 8. Pygmy squid are so small that they often cling to blades of sea-grass. 9. The octopus squid is known to detach its arms to distract predators. 10. Dumbo octopuses have large fins, which resemble the ears of the Disney-movie elephant. 11. The odd bobtail squid shoots out glow-in-the-dark mucus instead of ink. 12. Some species of young squid gather in groups of thousands to stay safe from predators. 13. Newborn cuttlefish are so small that four of them could fit inside a teaspoon. 14. Striped pajama squid spend most of their day hiding under sand on the seafloor. 15. When threatened, the blanket octopus unfurls long sheets of skin attached to its arms in order to appear bigger. 16. Dumbo octopuses live deeper in the sea than any other octopus—up to 23,000 feet below the surface. 17. After eating, many octopuses pile the empty shells of their prey outside their den. 18. The lyre cranch squid has eyes on long stalks. 19. The deadly blue-ringed octopus is the size of a golf ball, but it packs enough venom to kill 26 humans within minutes. 20. In certain light, a vampire squid's skin and eyes look deep red. 21. One ancient cephalopod had an 18-foot-long shell—that's longer than an SUV! 22. One captive octopus was so fond of a Mr. Potato Head toy that he fought back if anyone tried to take it away. 23. Mother octopuses carefully guard their eggs and gently push water over them to give them oxygen. 24. The deep-sea cockeyed squid has one bulging eye and one smaller eye. 25. The cockatoo squid holds its arms over its head, which makes it look like the bird it's named after. 26. Octopuses have three hearts—and blue blood! 27. Cuttlefish sometimes seem to hypnotize their prey by flashing colors and patterns. 28. A squid's brain is shaped like a doughnut. 29. Cephalopods' arms are attached to their heads. 30. Octopuses can usually fit through any space larger than their beak. 31. Squid have tube-shaped bodies, while cuttlefish have short, broad bodies. 32. Nautiluses are sometimes called "living fossils" because scientists think they have looked the same for millions of years. 33. Cephalopods dominated the seas for 400 million years—more than twice as long as dinosaurs roamed Earth! 34. Scientists have discovered the fossils of about 17,000 extinct cephalopod species. 35. There are more than 800 species of cephalopods alive today. 36. There are not many fossils of octopuses because their soft bodies don't preserve well. 37. An octopus can taste with its suckers. 38. The largest octopus suckers can each lift up to 30 pounds! 39. A giant Pacific octopus has about 2,000 suckers. 40. The edges of an octopus's suckers have microscopic grooves that help form a tight seal. 41. Squid can shoot out their tentacles in less time than it takes a human to blink.

42. The pygmy squid is so small it could fit on your fingernail—while the giant squid can be longer than a city bus. 43. One newly discovered tiny octopus species is so adorable that scientists may name it *adorabilis*. 44. Female argonauts can be 600 times bigger than males. 45. The giant squid's eyes are bigger than soccer balls! 46. The legendary kraken may have been based on the giant squid. 47. Some cephalopods have fins that help them steer. 48. Japanese flying squid can jet right out of the water. 49. Nautiluses usually swim backward, with their head and tentacles trailing behind them. 50. Chambered nautiluses can dive deeper than 2,000 feet without being crushed by the pressure. 51. A 600-pound octopus can squeeze through a tube the size of a quarter. 52. Captive octopuses sometimes climb into other tanks and eat their neighbors. 53. Octopuses sometimes crawl out of the water to hunt. 54. Most of an octopus's brain cells are in its arms. 55. Octopuses may use landmarks to find their way home. 56. Among invertebrates, cuttlefish have one of the largest brains for their body size. 57. Many cephalopods squirt ink to confuse predators. 58. Cephalopod ink may irritate predators' eyes and numb their sense of smell. 59. Some cuttlefish add ink to their eggs to help hide them. 60. In one experiment, cuttlefish mimicked a black-and-white checked pattern. 61. Squid can change their colors four times in a single second. 62. A cuttlefish's skin has more than 20 million pigment-filled cells. 63. To scare away predators, cuttlefish sometimes put a pair of spots on their back that look like eyes. 64. The mimic octopus can imitate stingrays, lionfish, and sea snakes. 65. Mimic octopuses protect themselves by posing as dangerous animals. 66. Pharaoh cuttlefish imitate hermit crabs to sneak up on their prey. 67. Some octopuses use six arms to imitate seaweed, while using the other two arms to walk away from danger. 68. Veined octopuses sometimes carry coconut shell halves to use as a shelter. 69. Some scientists believe that cuttlefish can count. 70. Some octopuses pile up rocks to block the entrance of their home. 71. One type of octopus may use jellyfish as tools to help catch more prey. 72. Cuttlefish can solve mazes. 73. Octopuses can learn to open childproof pill bottles. 74. One octopus juggled the hermit crabs in his tank for fun. 75. Giant cuttlefish are curious and will often come right up to divers. 76. Some squid can swim at speeds of up to 25 miles an hour—twice as fast as an Olympic champion! 77. Scientists have created an octopus-inspired material whose shape and texture can be changed on demand. 78. The average giant Pacific octopus can lay 90,000 eggs. 79. Giant squid use their long tentacles to snatch prey up to 33 feet away—that's almost the length of a bus! 80. The blanket octopus sometimes tears a stinging tentacle off a Portuguese man-of-war and uses it to fend off predators. 81. Some cephalopods live in the deepest part of the ocean, where there is no sunlight. 82. Every year, millions of firefly squid twinkle with glowing blue light in Japan's Toyama Bay. 83. Scientists think cuttlefish are actually color-blind! 84. Scientists believe that all octopuses are venomous. 85. An octopus's suckers grab by reflex, but a chemical in its skin keeps the suckers from sticking to the octopus by mistake. 86. Hawaiian bobtail squid coat their eggs in a jelly that contains bacteria. 87. Scientists are developing a robotic arm inspired by an octopus tentacle to help doctors perform surgeries. 88. A cuttlefish's eyes allow it to see what's in front of it and what's behind it at the same time. 89. Most adult cephalopods are solitary. But bigfin reef squid group together, possibly to look bigger to predators. 90. Humboldt squid have been spotted attacking sharks. 91. Most cephalopods live for only a year or two. 92. A cephalopod's beak is similar to a parrot's, but upside down. 93. Most octopuses hunt at night. But the day octopus hunts in the daytime. 94. Some cuttlefish use their arms to walk along the ocean floor. 95. All cephalopods have a rough-textured tongue called a radula. 96. Nautiluses sometimes eat shrimp and lobster shells to get nutrients that help them grow their own shells. 97. The word "octopus" comes from an ancient Greek word meaning "eight foot." 98. Some cuttlefish hide by burying themselves in the sand so that just their eyes poke out. 99. The two-spot octopus has blue spots near its head that look like an extra set of eyes. 100. Cephalopods have special organs called statocysts that help them balance underwater.

INDEX

Boldface indicates illustrations.

A
Ancient cephalopods 5, 12–13, **12–13**
Argonauts 19
Tentacles 4, 10, **10,** 16–17, **16–17,** 44

B
Brains 7, 28–29

C
Camouflage 30–37, **30–37**
Cephalopods
    bodies 14–27, **14–27**
    cool facts 4–5, **4–5,** 44–45, **44–45**
    intelligence 28–43, **28–43**
    introduction 6–13, **6–13**
Color changes 32–33, **32–33**
Cuttlefish
    arms and tentacles 10, **10,** 16, **16**
    color changes 7, **7,** 32–35
    cool facts 4–5, **5,** 44–45, **45**
    disguises 31, **31,** 34–37
    intelligence 29, **29,** 38, 40, 42

D
Disguises 30–37, **30–37**

E
Eggs 5, 19, 31, **31,** 44, **44,** 45
Eyes 4, 5, 20, 45, **45**
Eyes, fake 35, **35,** 45

F
Fossils 13, **13**

G
Giant cuttlefish 42
Giant Pacific octopuses 15, **15,** 19, 44
Giant squid 4, **4, 18,** 20–21, **20–21,** 44

H
Hearts 6
Humboldt squid 45, **45**

I
Ink 4, 5, 7, **30,** 30–31

Intelligence 28–43, **28–43**
Inventions inspired by octopuses 44, 45, **45**
Invertebrates 8, 20, 29

J
Japanese flying squid 23, **23**
Jet propulsion 22–23

M
Mimic octopuses 36–37, **36–37**

N
Nautiluses 11, **11,** 17, **17,** 24–25, **25,** 45

O
Octopuses
    cool facts 4–5, **4–5,** 44–45, **45**
    hearts 6, **6**
    intelligence 9, 28–29, **28–29,** 38–43,
      38–43
    size 19, **19**
    squeezing and escaping 9, **9,** 26–27, **26–27**
    suckers 14–15, **14–15,** 45

P
Pharaoh cuttlefish 37
Pigment 32–33
Pygmy squid 4, 18, **18**

S
Shells 11
Siphons 22, **22**
Squid
    arms and tentacles 4, 10, **10,** 16, **16**
    brains 7
    cool facts **4,** 4–5, 44–45, **45**
    jet propulsion 23, **23**
    size 18, **18,** 20–21, **20–21**
Suckers **14,** 16–17, 20, 45

T
Tentacles 4, 16–17, **16–17**
Tool use 39, **39**

V
Veined octopuses 38, **38,** 39, **39**

W
Whales 20, **20**